Published in 1999 by Creative Editions
123 South Broad Street, Mankato, Minnesota 56001
Creative Editions is an imprint of The Creative Company

Designed by Stephanie Blumenthal
Production Design by Melinda Belter
Editorial Assistance by Adele Richardson

Photographs by Richard Cummins, James Blank, Michelle Burgess, Don Eastman,
Beryl Goldberg, Janine Pestel, Tom Stack and Associates

Printed in United States of America

Library of Congress Cataloging-in-Publication Data

Willard, Keith
Skyscrapers / by Keith Willard
Includes index
Summary: Examines the history, design, construction, and uses of skyscrapers
and describes some notable examples.
ISBN 0-88682-719-1
1. Skyscrapers—Juvenile literature. [1. Skyscrapers.] I. Title.
TH1615.W55   1999
720'.483—dc21   98-18204

First Edition

2 4 6 8 9 7 5 3 1

SKYSCRAPERS

KEITH WILLARD

CREATIVE EDUCATION

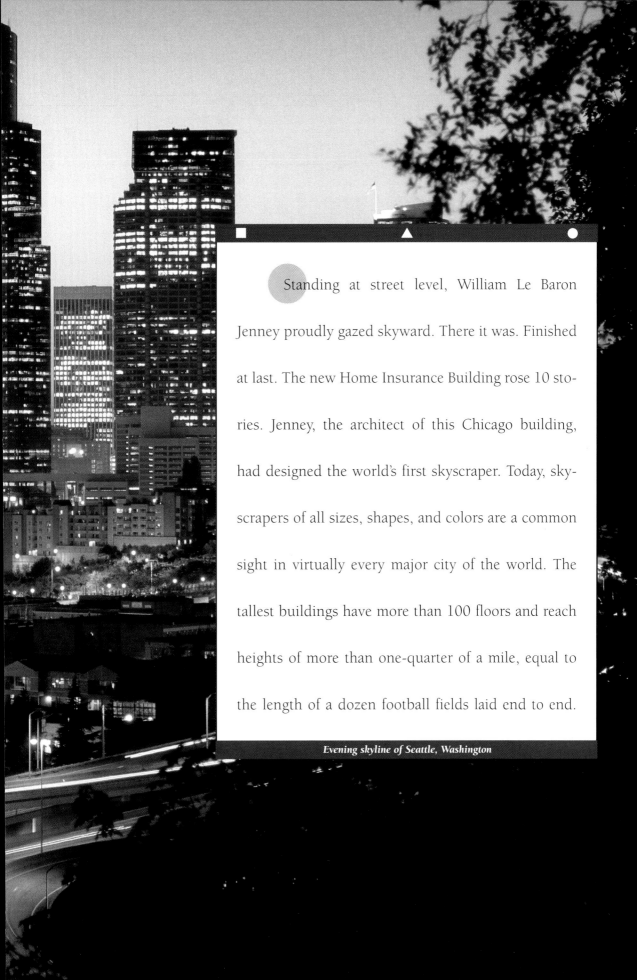

Standing at street level, William Le Baron Jenney proudly gazed skyward. There it was. Finished at last. The new Home Insurance Building rose 10 stories. Jenney, the architect of this Chicago building, had designed the world's first skyscraper. Today, skyscrapers of all sizes, shapes, and colors are a common sight in virtually every major city of the world. The tallest buildings have more than 100 floors and reach heights of more than one-quarter of a mile, equal to the length of a dozen football fields laid end to end.

Evening skyline of Seattle, Washington

From the top floor, maybe as many as 2,000 steps up, the view is magnificent. On a clear day a person can see for 80 miles (129 km) and even notice the curvature of the earth.

Large cities can often be identified by their unique skylines, but these tall towers scratching at the heavens are a fairly recent development.

The first skyscraper, the Home Insurance Building in Chicago, was completed in 1884. Architect William Le Baron Jenney built the first six floors using an iron framework, switching to steel for the last four. Steel worked so well that it has been used ever since.

Before the 1870s, skyscrapers didn't exist. Buildings were made of wood, brick, and stone and could only be constructed a few stories high.

Before the use of steel frames, walls held a structure up and could not safely support any additional weight beyond six floors. Masonry buildings required very thick walls

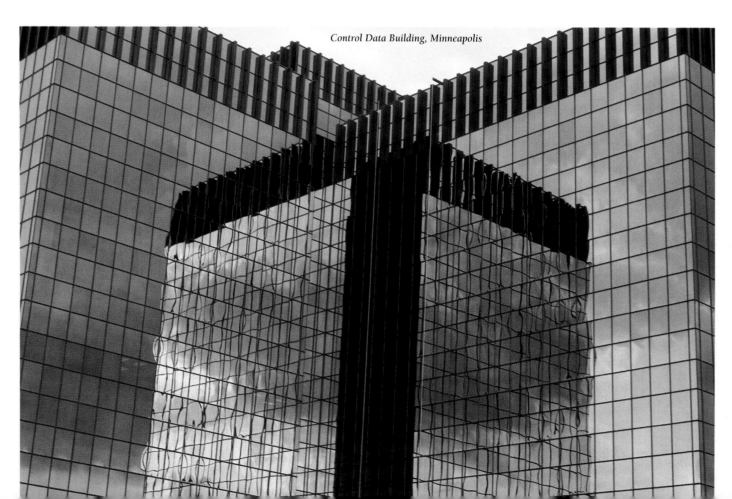

Control Data Building, Minneapolis

Skyscraper in Toronto, Canada

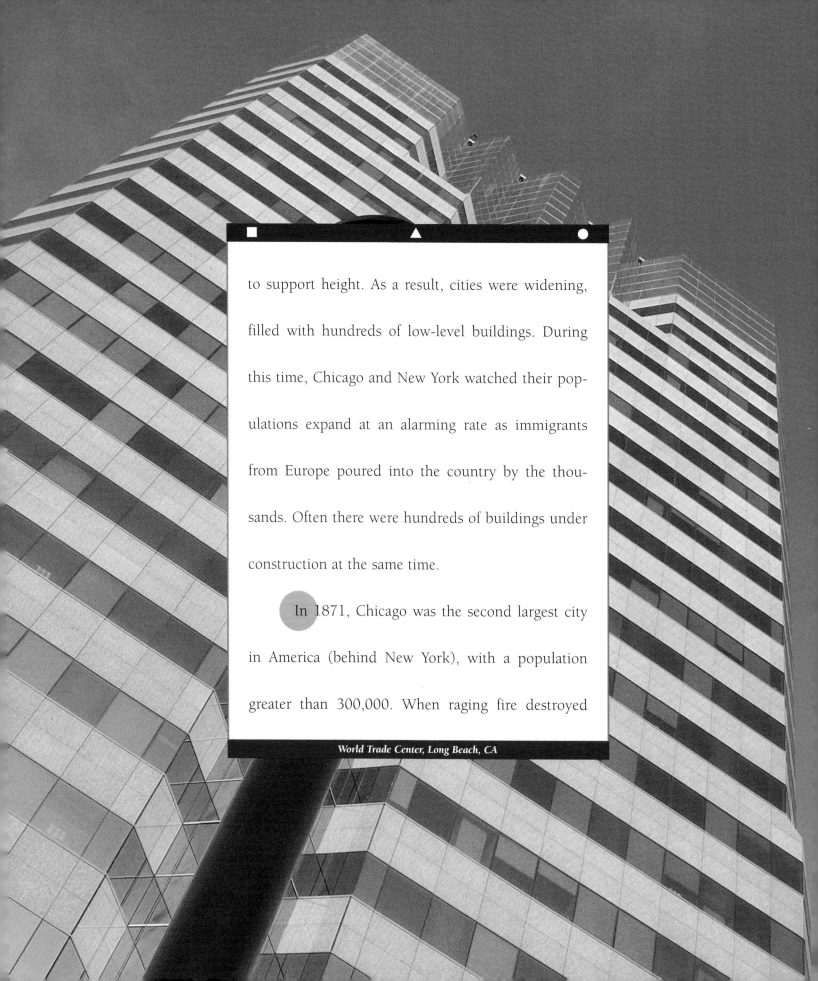

to support height. As a result, cities were widening,
filled with hundreds of low-level buildings. During
this time, Chicago and New York watched their pop-
ulations expand at an alarming rate as immigrants
from Europe poured into the country by the thou-
sands. Often there were hundreds of buildings under
construction at the same time.

In 1871, Chicago was the second largest city
in America (behind New York), with a population
greater than 300,000. When raging fire destroyed

World Trade Center, Long Beach, CA

more than one-third of the city that year, architects were hired from around the United States and Europe to prepare designs for new buildings—all as fireproof as possible. For these new structures, strong metal was used to create a skeleton, which, unlike simple walls, could support the weight of a building with many floors reaching higher and higher—the skyscraper.

In 1883, 12 years after the Great Chicago Fire, the Home Insurance Building was completed and the term "skyscraper" was first coined. Although the Home Insurance Building would be tiny by today's standards, at the time it was nearly twice the height of the surrounding structures. The Chicago building was torn down

Smith Tower and Interurban Buildings, Seattle

The Empire State Building in New York City was completed in 1931. Built in a little over one year, the construction is so solid that when an Army B-25 bomber crashed into the 79th floor in 1945, fire control was swift and the damage took only a short time to repair.

in 1931; however, the ideas it inspired in other architects would change the world, and its developing cityscapes, forever.

While the steel superstructure became the common means to support most buildings, the skeleton is not the most important part of a skyscraper. Without a solid foundation, a building must be limited in height.

Much of New York City sits on solid rock that can support buildings more than

A cloudy sky reflected in the glass skin of a skyscraper

1,000 feet (305 m) high. However, the tallest building in London is only 800 feet (244 m) because the city is built on clay, a softer foundation.

The type of foundation a building has depends greatly on the ground beneath it. Planners drill a hollow tube into the ground and pull up a sample. After they examine it closely, they determine the foundation needed. If the soil is firm, builders will construct a footing, where columns rest on a

G O I N G   U P

In very tall buildings, elevators can travel at speeds up to 1800 feet (550 m) per minute. That's the distance of 6 football fields.

Transamerican Pyramid and neighbor, San Francisco

Twin World Trade Towers dominate downtown New York City

small slab of concrete. Softer soil requires a raft foundation, which spreads the building's weight over a larger area. This type of foundation uses a continuous slab of concrete to make a platform which supports the whole building.

Another foundation type is based on the principle of buoyancy. Earth is removed from the building site that weighs as much or slightly less than the completed foundation will. Workers then build a floating foundation in the hole. If the ground is made of solid rock, or if the soil is unable to support the weight of the building, piles are driven into the earth and act like giant nails to anchor the building in place. A concrete platform is poured on top of the piles, and the superstructure is constructed on top of that. If a foundation has to be built underwater, below groundwater level, or in unstable soil, a box-like or cylindrical shell is built to protect workers from water and mud while working underground.

Once the foundation has been laid, the superstructure comes next. The framework for many

Lake Point Apartments, Chicago

Aerial view of the Empire State Building

skyscrapers is made of steel, but others have a reinforced concrete frame, supporting floors and walls with massive cement columns.

The first part of a skyscraper's superstructure to be built is the core. Large columns, which can be 20 feet (6 m) long and weigh more than 20 tons (18 metric tons), are set in

Detail on an art deco skyscraper

place by a huge crane. Once in place, girders are then bolted to the sides of the columns to form floor beams.

As the building rises, working a crane from the street level becomes impossible. A derrick may sit directly on the structure, or climbing tower cranes are raised from floor to floor.

Sunset reflected in the curved mirrors of a skyscraper

High rises disappear into the fog

While the frame continues to climb, work goes on below. Decking is attached to the floor beams and then covered with reinforced concrete. Plumbing, electrical wiring, cables, duct work, and telephone wires are run through tubes that hang on the underside of the decking.

Now the curtain walls can be attached. These are panels of concrete, thick glass, plastic, or some-times stainless steel that form the outer walls. These walls in no way support the building; they simply hang on the framework. Essentially, curtain walls are the "skin" of a skyscraper. Architects are always look-ing for new materials to use for curtain walls—any-thing that will give their building a more dramatic or unusual appearance.

Even after the curtain walls are in place,

workers continue to put in the ventilation system and electrical, plumbing, and phone lines. Now the elevators can also be installed, as well as the interior walls and ceiling panels. A coat of paint and some carpeting or tile will finish off the building floor by floor.

This kind of carefully planned interior design is important to the overall concept for a building, but what really catches the attention of a passerby is the building's exterior.

Early skyscraper architects used mostly classical

Dallas, Texas skyline

European styles with giant pillars, arches, and step-like exteriors. The Empire State Building is a good example of this style. It looks like a staircase for a giant as it rises from the base to the top of its antenna.

Art Deco style buildings appear to be carved out of single, tall blocks of material. New York City's Chrysler Building is a fine example of Art Deco. The tower of the Chrysler Building has triangular windows set between stainless steel arches. Around the

The Flatiron Building was built on a triangular-shaped lot

COMING THROUGH

In Miami, Florida an opening was designed in a building to allow a train to run completely through the structure.

Today's architecture reflects yesterday's

Woolworth Building, New York City

base of the tower are massive decorations modeled after the hood ornaments found on 1929 Chrysler automobiles. On top, the building sports a pyramid of stainless steel arched forms that taper upward to a stunning, sharp needle point.

Whereas Art Deco buildings may have had decoration near doors and windows, the glass-walled skyscrapers of the International Style completely avoided this type of ornamentation. Architect Ludwig Mies van der Rohe used the phrase "Less is more" to describe these buildings.

Post-modern architecture was developed in reaction to the International Style and was summed up by architect Robert Venturi with the phrase "Less is a

Many skyscrapers in earthquake-prone areas, such as California and Japan, have huge rubber springs under their foundations to absorb vibrations. These springs work in much the same way shock absorbers do on a car, so people feel fewer tremors.

bore." The AT&T building in New York City is an example of post-modern architecture. Completed in 1982, the building helped to define that style. Post-modern architecture also includes the more unusual, and sometimes even humorous, designs. The Space Needle in Seattle is a thin, round skyscraper that rises 600 feet (183 m). Hong Kong's Shanghai Bank has its support beams on the outside, giving it not only an unusual appearance, but a spacious interior. The 53rd At Third

The Chrysler Building's distinctive top

Philadelphia skyscraper

Building in New York is sometimes called "the lipstick building" because of its inspired design.

While Chicago might have started the skyscraper revolution, it was not the only city to recognize the advantages of building up. Most notable was New York City, which was quickly running out of space for its growing population and industries. By the end of the 19th century, New York had several skyscrapers. Two of the largest of that time were the American Surety Building with 21 floors and the Park Row Building with 29 floors. Park Row was completed in 1899 and captured the "world's tallest" title, towering 386 feet (118 m) in height. It would remain the tallest building in the world until 1913.

Other skyscrapers, which were not as tall but equally impressive, began sprouting up in other major cities. Washington, D.C. chose to be an exception, not allowing any structures to overshadow the Capital or the Washington Monument.

When the Woolworth Building in New York was completed in 1913, it broke the record for height. Built with 60 stories of beautiful Gothic ornamentation, it extended upward for 791 feet (241 m). Its finely detailed exterior topped with reaching spires gives it a breathtaking appearance. The build-

D E C O R A T I O N

Artificial lighting of skyscrapers is an architectural element used not only for practical purposes, but also for design.

Washington Mutual Tower, Seattle

ing, commissioned for Frank Win-field Woolworth, was paid for with 13.5 million dollars in cash. It has its own power plant and 28 high-speed elevators, the first of their kind. The building's record height remained unchallenged for 17 years.

When completed in 1958, New York's Seagram Building was considered the most luxurious skyscraper ever built. Everything inside, including the bathroom faucets was all custom made.

The Sears Tower in Chicago was then the world's tallest structure until 1996, when the Petronas Towers in Kuala Lumpur, Malaysia, were finished. Both buildings stretch upward 1,483 feet (452 m) and have shops, offices, and restaurants inside. They will remain the world's

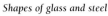

Shapes of glass and steel

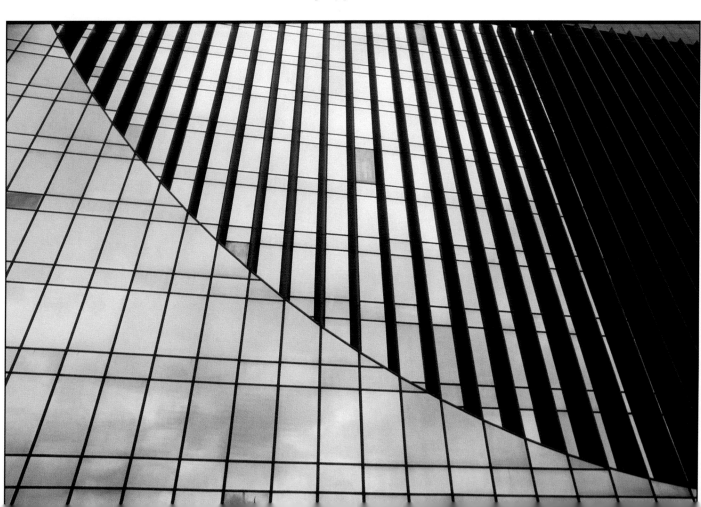

Interior of Hennepin County Building in Minneapolis

tallest only until new architectural marvels come along, including the World Financial Center under construction in Shanghai, China, which is projected to rise more than 1,500 feet (457 m) skyward.

For every skyscraper built, countless other designs have been pushed aside due to lack of funding. One of the most radical designs ever thought up was for a building to be called the Illinois. Designed by Frank Lloyd Wright in 1956, the Illinois was a dream that would shatter any record for height at 5,280 feet (1,609 m). Included in the design were two decks for 50 helicopters and 56 elevators using atomic-powered

New York, New York Casino in Las Vegas

engines. More than 130,000 people could have worked in it. Though it was never built, the Illinois still inspires architects to someday reach that mile-high mark.

The Millennium Tower, the brainchild of designer Sir Norman Foster, was proposed in 1989. The 2,755-foot (840 m) structure was to be built offshore, rising out of Japan's Tokyo Bay. Shaped like a huge needle, the building was planned as a home to nearly 50,000 people. Not only would there be apartments, but office space, hotels, and retail shops. In 1989, designer Cesar Pelli proposed the Miglen-Beitler Skyneedle to grace the Chicago skyline. Plans for

Nation's Bank in Miami

The Sears Tower in Chicago

construction were announced in 1990 with completion scheduled for 1994. Unfortunately, America's real estate market crashed in early 1991 due to the Persian Gulf War, and plans for the project were canceled. If built, the Skyneedle would have been the world's tallest building.

Another unrealized dream was the Chicago World Trade Center. Designed by Skidmore, Owings & Merrill (architects for the Sears Tower), the building

The Hancock Building in Boston

project would have continued if the 1.25 billion dollars needed in financing was secured. Rising 2,300 feet (701 m), the Center would have looked similar to the Sears Tower except for two giant holes in the upper frame of the building. The holes, measuring 60 feet (18 m) wide by 20 stories high, were designed to cut down on wind stress.

Even though none of these buildings ever

S Q U E A K Y   C L E A N

Window washers never finish their work on skyscrapers. By the time they are finished washing the last window, it's time to start all over again.

29

New San Francisco stands along old San Francisco

made it off the drawing board, there is little doubt that skyscrapers will continue to push the limits of size and design. Though no one can say how high skyscrapers can safely go, for architects and engineers, the possibilities are endless given the consistent advances in technology, construction materials, and building methods. As long as there are people who dream big, the cities of the world will be filled with buildings that scrape the sky.

Patterns of stone and glass

INDEX